Draw
BUILDINGS AND CITYSCAPES
Hans Schwarz

Series Editors: David and Brenda Herbert

ADAM & CHARLES BLACK · LONDON

Reprinted 1983
by A & C Black (Publishers) Ltd
35 Bedford Row, London WC1R 4JH

ISBN 0-7136-2331-4

First published 1980
by Pitman Publishing Ltd

Text set in VIP Palatino
Printed in Great Britain
by Hollen Street Press, Slough, Berkshire

Contents

Making a start

Learning to draw is largely a matter of practice and observation—so draw as much and as often as you can, and use your eyes all the time.

Look around you—at chairs, tables, plants, people, pets, buildings, your hand holding this book. Everything is worth drawing. The time you spend on a drawing is not important. A ten-minute sketch can say more than a slow, painstaking drawing that takes many hours.

Carry a sketchbook with you whenever possible, and don't be shy of using it in public, either for quick notes to be consulted later or for a finished drawing.

To do an interesting drawing, you must enjoy it. Even if you start on something that doesn't particularly interest you, you will probably find that the act of drawing it—and looking at it in a new way—creates its own excitement. The less you think about *how* you are drawing and the more you think about *what* you are drawing, the better your drawing will be.

The best equipment will not itself make you a better artist—a masterpiece can be drawn with a stump of pencil on a scrap of paper. But good equipment is encouraging and pleasant to use, so buy the best you can afford and don't be afraid to use it freely.

Be as bold as you dare. It's your piece of paper and you can do what you like with it. Experiment with the biggest piece of paper and the boldest, softest piece of chalk or crayon you can find, filling the paper with lines—scribbles, funny faces, lettering, anything—to get a feeling of freedom. Even if you think you have a gift for tiny delicate line drawings with a fine pen or pencil, this is worth trying. It will act as a 'loosening up' exercise. The results may surprise you.

Be self-critical. If a drawing looks wrong, scrap it and start again. A second, third or even fourth attempt will often be better than the first, because you are learning more about the subject all the time. Use an eraser as little as possible— piecemeal correction won't help.

Try drawing in colour. Dark blue, reddish-brown and dark green are good drawing colours. A coloured pencil, pen or chalk can often be very useful for detail, emphasis or contrast on a black and white drawing: for instance, in a street scene, draw the buildings in black, the people, car, etc. in another colour. This simple technique can be very effective.

You can learn a certain amount from copying other people's drawings. But you will learn more from a drawing done from direct observation of the subject or even out of your head, however stiff and unsatisfactory the results may seem at first.

A lot can be learned by practice and from books, but a teacher can be a great help. If you get the chance, don't hesitate to join a class—even one evening a week can do a lot of good.

Composition

Deciding where to place even the smallest sketch or doodle on a scribbling pad involves composition. It is generally best to make your drawing as large as possible on your piece of paper. But there are many possibilities. Sometimes you may not even want the whole of the object on your paper. And there is no reason why the paper should be the same shape as the subject—it is not, for instance, necessary to draw a tall object on an upright piece of paper.

When you are drawing more than one object on a sheet of paper, the placing of each object is also important. Try as many variations as possible.

Before you begin a drawing, think about how you will place it on the paper—even a few seconds' thought may save you having to start your drawing again. The simplest subjects can make good pictures. Most of the buildings and settings used in this book would not get a second glance from a passer-by, but all are worth drawing and some have made interesting compositions.

Before starting an elaborate drawing, do a few very rough sketches of the main shapes to help you decide on the final composition. When you have decided which to use, rule a faint network of lines—diagonal, vertical and horizontal—over this preliminary sketch and on the piece of paper to be used for the finished drawing. (Take care that both pieces of paper are the same proportion.) You will then have a number of reference points to enable you to transfer the composition to the final drawing.

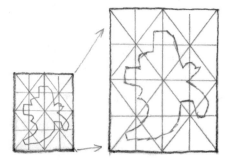

Rules are made to be broken. Every good artist is a good artist at least partly because of his originality; because he does what no one else has done before and because he breaks rules.

Every human being is unique. However poor an artist you *think* you are, you are different from everyone else and your drawing is an expression of your self.

What to draw with

Pencils are graded according to hardness, from 6H (the hardest) through 5H, 4H, 3H, 2H to H; then HB; then B, through 1B, 2B, 3B, 4B, 5B up to 6B (the softest). For most purposes, a soft pencil (HB or softer) is best. If you keep it sharp, it will draw as fine a line as a hard pencil but with less pressure, which makes it easier to control. Sometimes it is effective. to smudge the line with your finger or an eraser, but if you do this too much the drawing will look woolly. Pencil is the most versatile of all drawing techniques, suitable for anything from the most precise linear drawing to broad tonal treatment. Of course, a pencil line, even at its heaviest, is never a true black. But it has a lustrous, pewtery quality that is very attractive.

Charcoal can be bought in various qualities and sizes. I advise short sticks since they are cheaper, and long sticks soon break into short sticks anyhow.

Charcoal (which is soft and crumbly) is ideal for bold, large drawings. But beware of accidental smudging. Never rest your hand on the paper as you draw. If you are used to pen or pencil this may at first seem difficult. But you will soon get used to it and, once you do, will find it adds freedom and spontaneity to your work.

It is the most painterly of all drawing instruments. Smudging and erasing charcoal (traditionally done with kneaded pellets of bread) will give far more variety of texture than on a pencil drawing. And any part of the drawing you don't like can be removed with the flick of a rag. Take great care to preserve your successful drawings—by fixing them with a spray fixative (now universally sold in Aerosol cans), and by attaching to them an overlay of tissue paper.

Conté crayons, wood-cased or in solid sticks, are available in various degrees of hardness, and in three colours—black, red and white. The cased crayons are easy to sharpen, but the solid sticks are more fun—you can use the side of the stick for large areas of tone. Conté is harder than charcoal, but it is also easy to smudge. The black is very intense.

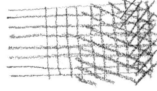

Reed, bamboo and quill pens are good for bold lines. You can make the nib end narrower or wider with the help of a sharp knife or razor blade. This kind of pen has to be dipped frequently into the ink.

Fountain pens have a softer touch than dip-in pens, and many artists prefer them. The portability of a fountain pen makes it a very useful sketching tool.

Special fountain pens, such as Rapidograph and Rotring, control the flow of ink by means of a needle valve in a fine tube (the nib). Nibs are available in several grades of fineness and are interchangeable.

The line they produce is of even thickness, but on a coarse paper you can draw an interesting broken line similar to that of a crayon. These pens have to be held at a right-angle to the paper, which is a disadvantage.

Inks also vary. Waterproof Indian ink quickly clogs the pen. Pelikan Fount India, which is nearly as black, flows more smoothly and does not leave a varnishy deposit on the pen. Ordinary fountain-pen or writing inks (black, blue, green or brown) are less opaque, so give a drawing more variety of tone. You can mix water with any ink in order to make it even thinner. But if you are using Indian ink, add distilled or rain water, because ordinary water will cause it to curdle.

Ball point pens make a drawing look a bit mechanical, but they are cheap and fool-proof and useful for quick notes and scribbles.

Fibre pens are only slightly better, and (whatever the makers say) their points tend to wear down quickly.

Felt pens are useful for quick notes and sketches, but not good for more elaborate and finished drawings.

9

Brushes are most versatile drawing instruments. The Chinese and Japanese know this and until recently never used anything else, even for writing. The biggest sable brush has a fine point, and the smallest brush laid on its side provides a line broader than the broadest nib. You can add depth and variety to a pen or crayon drawing by washing over it with a brush dipped in clean water.

Mixed methods are often pleasing. Try making drawings with pen and pencil, pen and wash, charcoal and wash, or Conté and wash. And try drawing with a pen on wet paper. Pencil and Conté do not look well together, and Conté will not draw over pencil or any greasy surface.

Above all, experiment with different techniques, on various qualities and surfaces, even if you quickly find a favourite way of doing things. A new technique will force you to vary the scale of your work and thus see it differently. A small circle, for example, looks different from a large one.

What to draw on

Try as many different surfaces as possible.

Ordinary, inexpensive paper is often as good as anything else: for example, brown and buff wrapping paper (Kraft paper) and lining for wallpaper have surfaces which are particularly suitable for charcoal and soft crayons. Some writing and duplicating papers are best for pen drawings. But there are many papers and brands made specially for the artist.

Bristol board is a smooth, hard white board designed for fine pen work.

Ledger Bond ('cartridge' in the UK) the most usual drawing paper, is available in a variety of surfaces—smooth, 'not surface' (semi-rough), rough.

Watercolour papers also come in various grades of smoothness. They are thick, high-quality papers, expensive but pleasant to use.

Ingres paper is mainly for pastel drawings. It has a soft, furry surface and is made in many light colours—grey, pink, blue, buff, etc.

Sketchbooks, made up from nearly all these papers, are available. Choose one with thin, smooth paper to begin with. Thin paper means more pages, and a smooth surface is best to record detail.

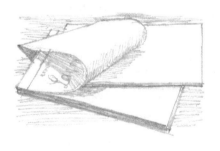

Lay-out pads make useful sketchbooks. Although their covers are not stiff, you can easily insert a stiff piece of card to act as firm backing to your drawing. The paper is semi-transparent, but this can be useful—almost as tracing paper—if you want to make a new improved version of your last drawing.

An improvised sketchbook can be just as good as a bought one—or better. Find two pieces of thick card, sandwich a stack of paper, preferably of different kinds, between them and clip together at either end.

Perspective

You can be an artist without knowing anything about perspective. Five hundred years ago, when some of the great masterpieces of all time were painted, the word did not even exist. But most beginners want to know something about it in order to make their drawings appear three-dimensional rather than flat, so here is a short guide.

The further away an object is, the smaller it seems.

All parallel horizontal lines that are directly opposite you, at right-angles to your line of vision, remain parallel.

All horizontal lines that are in fact parallel but go away from you will appear to converge at eye-level at the same vanishing point on the horizon. Lines that are *above* your eye-level will seem to run downwards towards the vanishing point; lines that are *below* your eye-level will run upwards. You can check the angles of these lines against a pencil held horizontally at eye-level.

The larger and closer any object is, the bigger the front of it will seem to be in relation to the part furthest away, or to any other more distant object. Its actual shape will appear foreshortened or distorted. A matchbox close to you will appear larger and more distorted than a distant house, and if you are drawing a building seen at an angle through a window, the window frame will be larger and more distorted than the building.

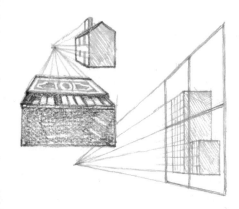

If the side of an object is facing you, one vanishing point is enough (as in the matchbox drawing); but if the corner is facing you, two vanishing points will be needed.

It may even be necessary to use three vanishing points when your eye is well above or below an object, but these occasions are rare.

Diagonal lines drawn between the opposite angles of a square or rectangle will meet at a point which is half-way along its length or breadth. This remains true when the square or rectangle is foreshortened. You may find it helpful to remember this when you are drawing surfaces with equal divisions—for example, a tiled floor or the divisions between window panes—or deciding where to place the point of a roof or the position of windows on a façade.

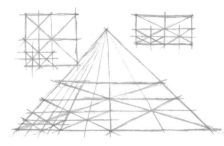

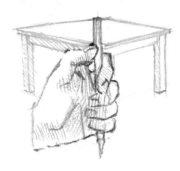

You will tend to exaggerate the apparent depth of top surfaces because you know they are square or rectangular and want to show this in your drawing.

You can check the correct apparent depth of any receding plane by using a pencil or ruler held at eye-level and measuring the proportions on it with your thumb. If you use a ruler you can actually read off the various proportions.

One point to mention again: *all* receding parallel lines have the same vanishing point. So if, for instance, you draw a street this will apply to all the horizontal edges—roofs, doors, windows, lines of bricks, chimneys.

Drawings with a single vanishing point

Try a single small building to begin with—the front seen flat on, the side foreshortened. The diagram shows how *all* parallel lines run to the same vanishing point, whether the lines are the edges of big shapes or of single bricks. If they run parallel, they converge at the same spot on the horizon, on your eye-level.

I have drawn this with a Rotring (Rapidograph) pen. Fine fibre-pens give similar effects.

Here I used a black crayon. A soft pencil, 2B or softer, would have looked much the same. The tone—shadow—makes the drawing look more solid. Notice how different areas of shadow vary in darkness and that I have avoided solid blacks.

The perspective diagram again demonstrates that *all* parallel lines share *one* vanishing point.

The next five pages show how this, the simplest perspective scheme—with one vanishing point—can be used for quite elaborate drawings.

Getting more complicated, but still using only one vanishing point.

Dividing a rectangle which you *see* in perspective by diagonals gives you the *apparent* half-way point. This is what I did to get the perspective correct for the windows on the left in this top drawing— dividing the halves again by diagonals to make a division into four.

In the second drawing the shop window on the right has also been halved by diagonals (see perspective diagram). Notice how very much wider the near half appears.

All the drawings on this page were done with an HB pencil.

The effectiveness of this drawing depends on the contrast between the large railings in the foreground and the small-scale detail in the background. It was made with a Chinagraph pencil.

The diagram shows how drawing diagonals over the sloping rectangle formed by the five bridge-supports gives you the half-way point, and diagonals of the two halves give you the spacing of the struts—as with the spacing of the windows on the previous page.

The drawing below also has a single vanishing point – just above the tree-tops and to the left of the centre trees. The perspective is so simple that a diagram is not needed.

The trees and some of the doors and windows were drawn with a broad Rotring pen, the rest of the buildings and the figures with a fine one. A worn and a new fibre-pen would give similar effects.

The contrast between the bold, free textures of the trees and the stiff geometric pattern of the buildings is the basis of the composition. The figures add life to the scene and give scale to the drawing. They also emphasise the contrast between the stiff upper half of the drawing and the free lower half, and at the same time carry the finer texture of the buildings into the lower part.

The distances between the barn-supports has again been worked out by drawing in the diagonals—which, next to drawing the vanishing point is the most useful perspective device. The darker, bolder tones were drawn with a Chinagraph crayon, the lighter textures with a hard black crayon.

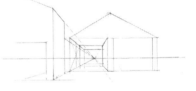

The small diagrams show four compositions based on the same view. The simplest subjects contain innumerable composition possibilities. By moving your own position left or right a few feet, or by standing higher up or sitting lower down, you can increase these possibilities even further.

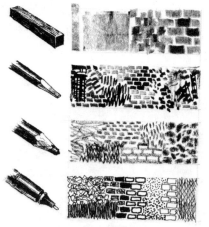

Here, too, there is a single vanishing point—near the base of the most distant building on the right. The drawing is an exercise in textures and techniques. I have used the following:

Black oil-pastel—Laid on its side for shading, and with the square end drawing individual bricks (one line, one brick).

The handle of a watercolour brush, cut to a chisel-edge and used as a pen. This can produce a fine line or, if used broad-on, can draw individual bricks in one line. In use and effect it is similar to reed and bamboo pens.

A Chinagraph crayon

Two different weights of Rotring pens

Drawings with two vanishing points

Here, I go back to perspective and the subject of my first drawing on p. 14—this time there are two vanishing points. The first diagram explains their use.

The second diagram, at first sight complicated, shows the perspective of the roof. By drawing diagonals at the base of the roof I have first established the centre. By linking intermediate points along the diagonals, and drawing verticals from the points of intersection to where they (in turn) meet the slope of the roof, I have arrived at the base-line of the structure on top.

The last diagram provides help for the drawing of arches. It shows the basic construction of a circle seen in perspective. Draw a square, put in the diagonals, then quarter it. Finally, draw an oval, touching the square only at the four quartered points.

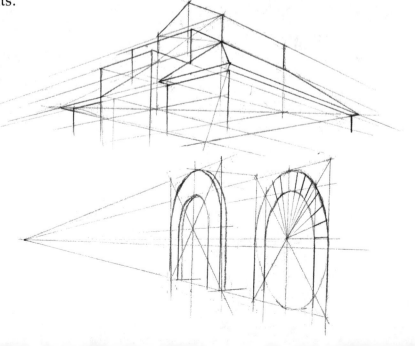

Drawn with a broad-nibbed Rotring pen, here is the second building from p. 14—again using two vanishing points.

The dark buildings on the left make the light roof and wall of the foreground building look luminous by contrast; compare the treatment on p. 14 where the light wall is against white paper.

The diagram shows how the roof was constructed by drawing diagonals on its base-rectangle. Verticals from the resulting centre-line provide the points where the roof-slopes meet.

More advanced exercises

Here, I used a black wax-crayon for flat over-all tones and reflections on the wet pavement, and a Rotring pen for paving and other detail.

No fewer than nine vanishing points were established in the diagram: two for the building and the steps, three for the paving-stones, one for the trees, and three for the balustrade. This is not as complicated as it sounds, as all perspective lines are horizontal, and all vanishing-points spaced along the horizon at eye-level. Once again, the arch was constructed on the principle of establishing diagonals, and halving.

Here for the first time there is a vanishing point *not* on your eye-level. The road leading upwards on the left, not being a horizontal plane, has its vanishing-point *above* the horizon. Everything else—walls, pillar, train-shed, buildings, the courses of bricks—being horizontal or defined by horizontal lines or edges, has its vanishing point on the horizon.

But what is getting more important than perspective is the subjects of your drawings. This, and other pages, show that it does not need an obviously picturesque view to make a picture.

The drawing was done with a brush-handle pen and a fine Rotring pen.

This drawing, too, was done with a brush-handle pen. For the fine lines, I held it edgeways or angled so that only a corner of it touched the paper. For the grey lines I dipped the drying pen into water, and the chalk-like textured lines were drawn with the drying pen.

The perspective gets more complicated. The building on the right and the steps on the far left share one vanishing point at eye-level. The slope of the steps and the steeper sections of the balustrade share one too, but well *above* eye-level. The less steep sections of the balustrade and the lane on the right share a third vanishing point, again above the horizon.

Buildings, streets, towns, do not consist only of straight lines, sharp angles, cubes, rectangles. Here, curves form the basis of the design—a curved road, an arched workmen's shelter, arched and circular windows, echoed and re-inforced by barrow and tar-drums.

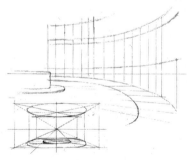

As with arches on earlier pages, a circle inscribed in a square is helpful for large, horizontal curves. The diagram explains the principle—with circles at ground-level below and circles above the horizon.

Remember that the centre of a circle in perspective appears well beyond half-way between front and back of the oval. Therefore, lines which radiate from the centre of the circle—in this case the lines of the paving-stones—do not run to the *geometric* centre of the oval. Notice also how wide the pavement appears at the side and how narrow at the back, where the oval flattens.

A hardish black crayon was used for the main drawing.

Drawing by stages: a single building

1 Although proportion and perspective were my first consideration, tone is also indicated at the beginning to help me see the shape more clearly and to give me some idea of the ultimate composition. At this stage, keep everything simple and fluid.

2 The whole drawing becomes firmer. Details, such as windows, are added, and tone developed. Since my final picture will be heavy in tone, I know that the construction lines I have drawn in (from centres of gables, along lines of windows) will be absorbed later. Don't spend time fussily putting in and erasing 'wrong' lines.

3 Here too the picture has been worked on all over. Notice that I have added some very strong tones to demonstrate how far I can ultimately go.

4 This is the finished drawing, made with a 2B pencil— showing final refinements, such as architectural detail, texture on walls, elaboration of sky. The heavy tones, so noticeable in the previous stage, have now been absorbed in the general scheme. The houses have been left light, in contrast to the church—which is the real subject of the drawing.

Drawing by stages: a cityscape

These four sketches demonstrate the following points:

Start with the main shapes. If you intend to use tone, do so from the start; if strong tone, put some in early.

A drawing should not look incomplete at any stage.

With mixed techniques—here Chinagraph and two widths of Rotring pens—bring in your whole range at an early stage. Do not complete a line drawing with a pencil, then trace the line with a pen; it will lead to dead, mechanical drawing.

If the final drawing is bold, it will absorb early mistakes. Do not constantly erase or timidly re-draw.

It is easy to over-elaborate a drawing—you may prefer the third stage here to the finished version.

Draw in all small detail—lettering, windows etc.—right at the end. Keep the drawing as simple as you can for as long as you can.

From first sketch to finished drawing

The contrast between the white house and the dark buildings framing it was the inspiration for this drawing—done with Chinagraph and litho chalk. So, I first settled the shape of the light building, and then immediately isolated it by indicating the tone on the rest of the drawing. One good, interesting *big* shape is worth more than a lot of interesting *small* detail.

Street furniture and street life

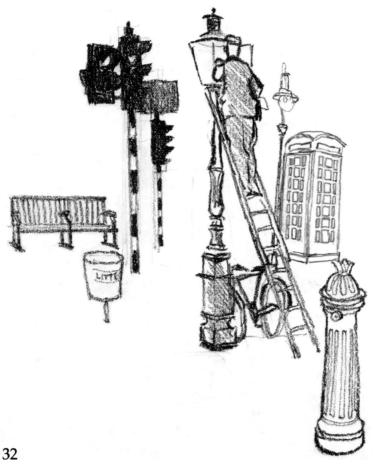

Benches, lamp-posts, bollards—what is known as street furniture—add to the liveliness of an urban setting. Cars, buses, trucks, motorbikes are always with us and can also add interesting detail.

This drawing, done at speed with a fine Rotring pen, pays little heed to correct perspective and may be better for it.

Every town or city offers a variety of events and activities in its streets: processions, buildings in progress, children's play-grounds, markets.

The top drawing is a
street-market in London,
made with a black
crayon. It would be very
empty without the people
and street furniture,
which are the real subject
of the drawing.

The second scene is a
Spanish market, drawn
with a broad Rotring pen.
I have tried to suggest
harsh light by using a
dazzle-pattern of black
and white, without
putting in realistic light
and shade.

33

Same subjects/ different techniques

Look out of the nearest window and you will see something worth drawing. I hope that the drawings on the next six pages prove this.

The four here were all made from the same window in my house. They are all segments of the same roof-scape.

The first—drawn with a fine Rotring pen—gives prominence to the textures and tones of bricks and tiles. The second—drawn with a black crayon—does the same thing but this time in a linear style; but it is the contrast between two vertical shapes—the chimney and chimney-pots in the foreground and the church-steeple in the background—which is the real subject of the drawing. Notice that, for the sake of balance, the sky is treated as a texture.

The subject of the first drawing here—made with a 4B pencil—is a very small section of my view. Notice the staggered repeat-pattern of the chimneys. The window in the centre on its patch of light wall is a focus and steadying element of the composition.

The bottom drawing, done with my brush-handle pen, is a near-panoramic view. Fine detail is ignored to stress the strong black/white pattern. Here the sky is important, and takes up nearly two thirds of the drawing. Its free, atmospheric treatment contrasts with the block-like buildings and adds depth and distance.

The same view in sunshine and in rain. The sunny
one—drawn with a broad Rotring pen—the rainy one with
fibre-pens, show how similar are the effects of these two
instruments. For the chalk-like effects in the rain scene, I held
the fibre-pen at a sloping angle; for the fine lines in the
background I used a new, still sharply-pointed pen, and for
the foreground an older, blunter pen.

Notice the variety of treatment in repetitive rows of windows
or chimneys.

The dazzle of sunlight hides foreground detail, whereas mist,
rain, and relative darkness flatten and obscure distance;
compare the two drawings in this respect.

Different subjects/different techniques

I drew the attractive early 19th century houses (above) in the style of an architect's elevation, with fibre-pen and Chinagraph pencil, free-hand, but using a ruler and set square for the preliminary pencil layout. A ruler can be used for a final drawing too, provided it does not lead to over-timidity and fussiness. I deliberately ignored light and shade, to give full weight to windows, railings, tiles and brick-textures.

The bottom drawing—made with a B pencil—uses tone and texture to emphasise the solidness of the piled-up bulk of the houses rising through and above foliage and trees.

Here are two drawings with strong dark/light contrasts. The first—made with a 3B pencil—shows how somewhat stark modern buildings can be treated imaginatively and freely. Note, for instance, the varying treatment of the windows.

Below: an overnight snow-fall turned what is a normally dull view of mean municipal housing into an exciting pattern.

Often snow is appreciably lighter than the sky, but when I did this drawing, roof and sky were the same tone. Chimneys and gables give enough hints about size and slope of roofs to make further definition unnecessary.

Most other surfaces seemed to have a nearly-even dark tone, so I brought forward the nearer houses by using coarser textures.

39

Industrial subjects

Industrial areas include particularly varied structures. In the first drawing, every shape is different. With a B pencil, I have used what is known as aerial perspective—the further away, the lighter the tone.

The second drawing, of a cement-mixing plant, brings out solidness by linear perspective only—the kind I dealt with in the early part of the book.

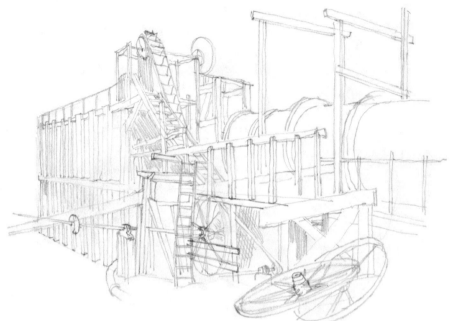

In the pen drawing below distance is indicated by the contrast between the delicate treatment of the background screen of factories and warehouses and the lines of the staging. The larger black areas help to bring the staging forwards.

The individual shapes of these factory buildings are simple and basic. The variety of their scale and size justify this slight pencil drawing.

Railways with their gantries, sheds, bridges, are similar to industrial subjects. The second drawing here shows their urban aspect—the entrance to a main-line station. The figures drawn in different weights with fibre-pens provide an impression of bustle and liveliness.

Constrast the third pencil-drawing of a sleepy rural station. Its effect relies on echoes and contrasts between left and right halves of the drawing: the roof against the similar sloping shape of the foreshortened balustrade; the horizontals of platform and rails against the parallel lines of the steps.

41

Parks and spaces

Top: a drawing of buildings seen *from* a park. The informal, non-geometric character of bench, chairs and railings contrasts with the geometric forms behind.

Left: A tea-pavilion and fountain, which are formal (symmetrical) are given a holiday mood by the casual figures and light linear technique.

Right: A tea-shack with lively lettering, boarding and accidental shapes.

Both drawings on this page were made with fibre-pens. For the second, I added simple tone with a Chinagraph pencil to three flat areas—trees, grass and table reflections. Notice that the trees are shown as one unit—a massed canopy, supported by trunks, whose diminishing sizes provide distance.

Above: Pencil drawing of 18th century gravestones.

Below: A building site whose confused tangle and vitality I have tried to reproduce by means of strong tonal contrast, using brush-handle pen and Chinagraph.

Architectural details

Draw from nature if you can, but these details were taken from photographs and still have a certain liveliness.

Finished drawings/ contrasting techniques

Below: Strong tone and free textures, created with a brush-handle pen; for the lighter lines I dipped my near-dry pen into water.

Opposite: A fine Rotring pen gives equal emphasis to bricks, cobbles, railings, glazing-bars, producing a flat all-over pattern. Light and shade, tone, colour, depth were ignored to produce the spidery, but lively texture.

This drawing is only concerned with a tonal pattern based on the effects of sunlight. Any detail which may have weakened this was sacrificed. Notice the limited use of the heaviest tones; a constant sledge-hammer contrast of black-and-white is not necessary to get an effect of sunlight. I made the drawing with black crayon, mostly with the crayon laid on its side and dragged across the paper.

In this book I have suggested a variety of approaches to the subject—all of them, obviously, within my own ability and outlook. Experience and constant looking and drawing will develop *your* approach. The possibilities are endless.